Disability PRIDE

Technology Matters

Jeni Vasquez

PowerKiDS press

Published in 2026 by The Rosen Publishing Group, Inc.
2544 Clinton Street, Buffalo, NY 14224

First Edition

Editor: Danielle Haynes
Book Design: Leslie Taylor

Photo Credits: Cover, p. 5 Wavebreak Media ltd/Alamy.com; (series background) P.siripak/Shutterstock.com; (series disability pride colors) rudall30/Shutterstock.com; p. 5 magda_shutterstock/Shutterstock.com, (flag sidebar) Maxim Studio/Shutterstock.com; p. 7 Lisa F. Young/Shutterstock.com; p. 9 myboys.me/Shutterstock.com; p. 11 LightField Studios/Shutterstock.com; p. 13 zlikovec/Shutterstock.com; p. 15 Reshetnikov_art/Shutterstock.com; p. 17 Vergani Fotografia/Shutterstock.com; p. 19 Pressmaster/Shutterstock.com, p. 21 metamorworks/Shutterstock.com.

Library of Congress Cataloging-in-Publication Data

Names: Vasquez, Jeni author
Title: Technology matters / Jeni Vasquez.
Description: [Buffalo] : PowerKids Press, [2026] | Series: Disability pride | Includes bibliographical references and index.
Identifiers: LCCN 2025034883 | ISBN 9781499457131 library binding | ISBN 9781499457124 paperback | ISBN 9781499457148 ebook
Subjects: LCSH: Technology and people with disabilities–Juvenile literature
Classification: LCC HV1568 .V38 2026 | DDC 362.400285-dc23/eng/20250912
LC record available at https://lccn.loc.gov/2025034883

Manufactured in the United States of America

Some of the images in this book illustrate individuals who are models. The depictions do not imply actual situations or events.

CPSIA Compliance Information: Batch #CWPK26. For Further Information contact Rosen Publishing at 1-800-237-9932.

Contents

Part of Your Life

Technology is a huge part of many people's everyday lives. Its role, or part, in the world has grown a lot even in your lifetime, and it will likely continue to grow more in many ways. Most people in the United States use modern technology a lot, and this, of course, includes people with many different disabilities.

Many people with disabilities and their **allies** are working to make modern technology more **accessible** to everyone, including those with different **physical** and **intellectual** disabilities. In addition, there are many ways that some kinds of tech can help people with disabilities and make life easier and better.

The disability pride flag was created to show acceptance and respect for people who have disabilities. Each color is for a different type of disability.

- The gray background is in honor of those who've died.
- Green is for disabilities that have to do with the senses.
- Blue is for those that have to with the mind and emotions.
- White stands for unseen disabilities, as well as those that haven't been diagnosed, or found out.
- Gold is for **neurodiversity**.
- Red is for other disabilities of the body.

A smartphone is a key piece of technology many people use these days. As of 2025, about 97 percent of people in the United States have one.

What Is Technology?

In its simplest form, technology is a method that uses science to solve problems and the tools used to solve those problems. Things as simple as screws or wheels are forms of technology. However, when people talk about technology today, they often mean devices such as computers, tablets, and smartphones and other things that connect to the internet.

These devices aren't just a fun way to pass the time with games and memes and chatting, although they're certainly that too. They're a big part of job skills and everyday life. Sometimes, the only place you can get things like bus times is online. You must apply to many jobs online too.

While many people have smartphones or computers, not everyone does. It's important to remember that many libraries have public computers that you can use.

Learn More

Braille is a writing system used by people who are blind. It was invented by Louis Braille, who was blind, in 1824.

Accessibility

There are a few different ways that technology needs to be accessible to those with disabilities. People with physical disabilities may need devices they can control without using their hands. People who are blind or have trouble seeing may need devices that have braille keyboards or displays or **software** to read on-screen words out loud.

Sometimes accessibility means addressing further issues that people without disabilities (or those with other disabilities) might not think of. Websites that aren't coded well may cause problems for screen readers or software—so can unusual **fonts** on websites. These can also cause issues for those with learning issues such as dyslexia.

It’s important to remember that not all disabilities are visible, or can be seen. This includes dyslexia and other learning disorders.

Learn More

Dyslexia is a learning disorder affecting how people deal with language, especially reading and spelling. It often runs in families.

Another way in which technology needs to be accessible to those with disabilities is in education. Sometimes, people **assume** that those with disabilities can't learn to use different kinds of technology. This is often true of those with intellectual and **developmental** disabilities. But disabilities don't mean that people can't learn, just that they may have to learn in different ways or need a little more help.

It's not good to assume things about people with disabilities, even if you have disabilities yourself. Everyone is different! Some organizations, or groups, are working to provide technology coaching to those who need it today.

Learn More

In 2010, President Barack Obama signed the Twenty-First Century Communications and Video Accessibility Act. This law works to make sure that modern technology is more available and accessible to those with disabilities.

Better-designed computer interfaces help everyone, not just those with disabilities.

Getting an Assist

So, it's good to make sure the same devices can be used by many different kinds of people, including those with many different disabilities. But even with this, it's also good to have other devices and software that are particularly meant for those with different disabilities. These are called assistive technologies.

Some of these meant to help people use computers include **text**-to-speech software, software that can make what's on the screen bigger, different kinds of keyboards, braille displays or printers, and computer mouses that people with low hand or wrist **mobility** can use with their feet.

This person is using a braille keyboard and display. The dots lift and lower to spell out words in braille.

Learn More

At least 15 percent of the world's people have at least one disability. The U.S. Centers for Disease Control and Prevention (CDC) says that about 1 in 4 residents of the United States have a disability.

Beyond Computers

Of course, there are many kinds of technology that can help people with disabilities with things that have nothing to do with using computers. Wheelchairs are a kind of technology! In fact, the wheel was likely one of the earliest forms of tech. Today's wheelchairs, however, can be far more than just chairs with wheels. Some can go on all kinds of terrain, or ground, or have their own **navigation** systems.

Glasses and hearing aids are kinds of technology! So are prostheses, or man-made devices to replace part of the body. There is also assistive software of many kinds.

Learn More

Sometimes people who can't speak in other ways will use devices they control to speak for them. Scientist Stephen Hawking used a device like this.

Prostheses have come a long way. Some can be made on a 3D printer and updated as you grow!

An App for That

Smartphone apps are a kind of software. In recent years, people have created hundreds of apps to help those with different kinds of disabilities. Many of these creators have disabilities themselves, and many apps are cheap or even free. Because they run on small devices, they can be very useful!

There are apps that help people with ADHD manage their time and apps that help them focus, or pay attention. Some apps help people with brain fog remember things. There are apps that help people find wheelchair-accessible restaurants, stores, and other places. Apps can even help people manage pain and track symptoms, or signs, of illness.

Some apps can give users a transcript, or written record, of what another person is saying. This can help those who are deaf or hard of hearing.

AI and Access

Artificial intelligence, or AI, is the ability of a machine to copy intelligent human behavior. People can use it in many ways, including to help with disability issues. It can collect information, or facts (although it's best to be sure they come from good sources), for people who have trouble handling a lot of searches. It can give people a way to, in part, create art when they have no other way to do so.

There are many concerns about AI, however. There are many signs that much AI has biases, or unfair ways of thinking, including biases about those with disabilities.

Learn More

Because of the information that's trained it, AI can assume what's "normal," or usual, or use stereotypes, or commonly held ideas about people that aren't always true. It's important to be careful about this.

AI can be trained to learn a person's unique speech habits—which may be affected by a disability—so they can use voice-activated devices and speech-to-text technology.

Living Life

While there are some concerns about types of technology, as a whole, it can help the lives of people with disabilities in many ways. It's important to make sure that modern technology is accessible to everyone, because it's a big part of life now, and that's not changing.

In the future, AI may help with even more technology, including self-driving cars that could help those who can't drive themselves. While we should be careful of some aspects, or parts, of this, it's also good to see how much it can help us all live life to the fullest!

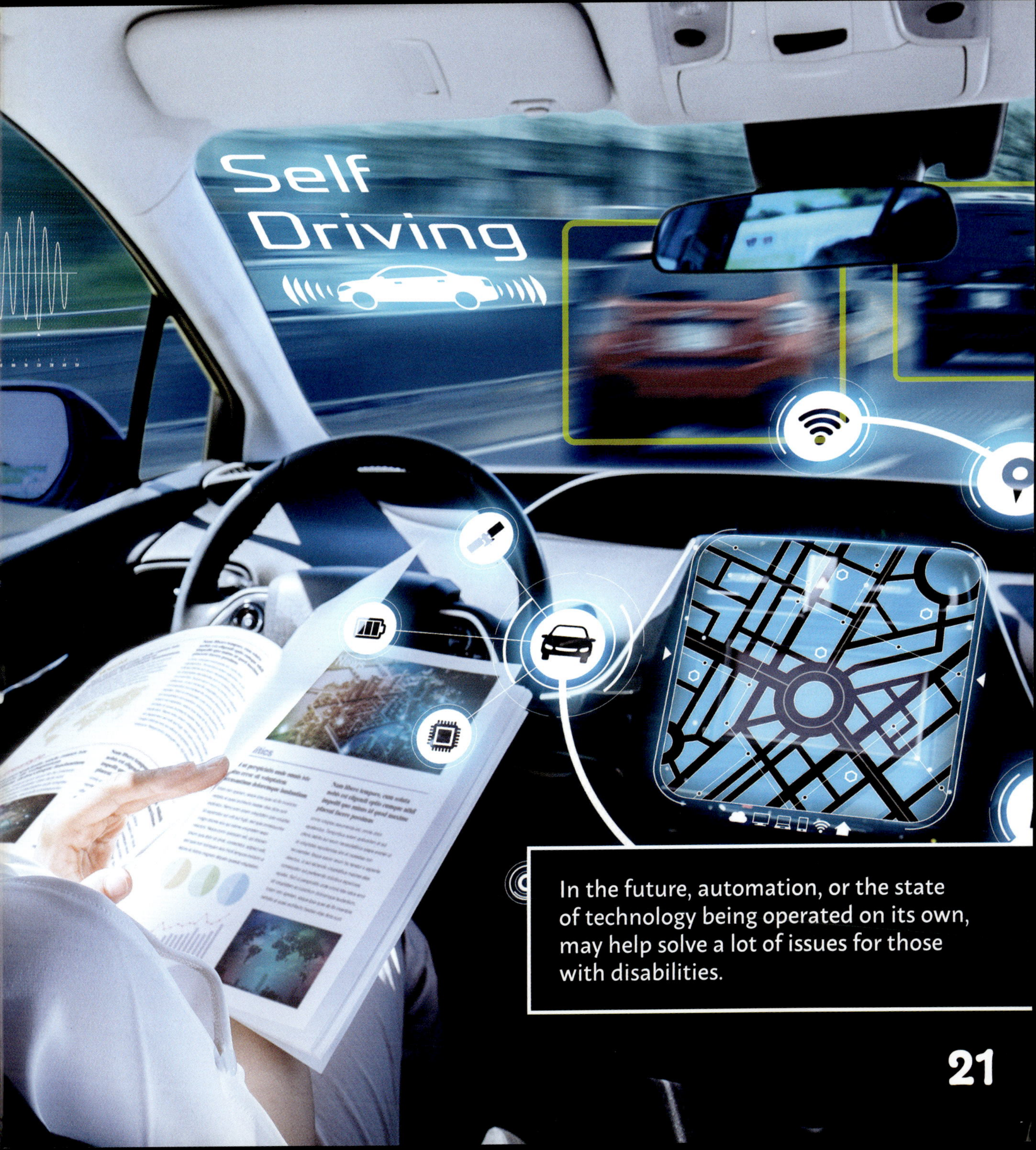

In the future, automation, or the state of technology being operated on its own, may help solve a lot of issues for those with disabilities.

Glossary

accessible: Able to obtain, use, get into, or understand.

ally: A person associated with another for support or a common purpose.

assume: To take something as granted or true.

developmental: Having to do with development, or the act of growing and changing.

font: A set of characters for writing; for example, those on a computer program.

intellectual: Relating to intellect, or the power of thinking or knowing.

mobility: The ability to move or be moved.

navigation: The act or process of finding the way to get to a place when you are traveling.

neurodiversity: Differences in the way the brain processes information.

physical: Relating to the body instead of the mind.

software: Programs that run on computers and perform certain functions.

text: The words of a printed or written work.

For More Information

BOOKS

Hawking, Lucy, and Stephen Hawking. *You and the Universe.* New York, NY: Random House, 2024.

Kaminski, Leah. *Bionic Bodies.* Fremont, CA: Full Tilt Press, 2021.

WEBSITES

Dyslexia

my.clevelandclinic.org/health/diseases/6005-dyslexia
Learn more about this learning issue at the Cleveland Clinic website.

Wheelchairs

kidshealth.org/en/kids/wheelchairs.html
Learn more about modern wheelchairs on this website.

Index